W0091258

Discover India
State by State

OFF TO BIHAR

SONIA MEHTA

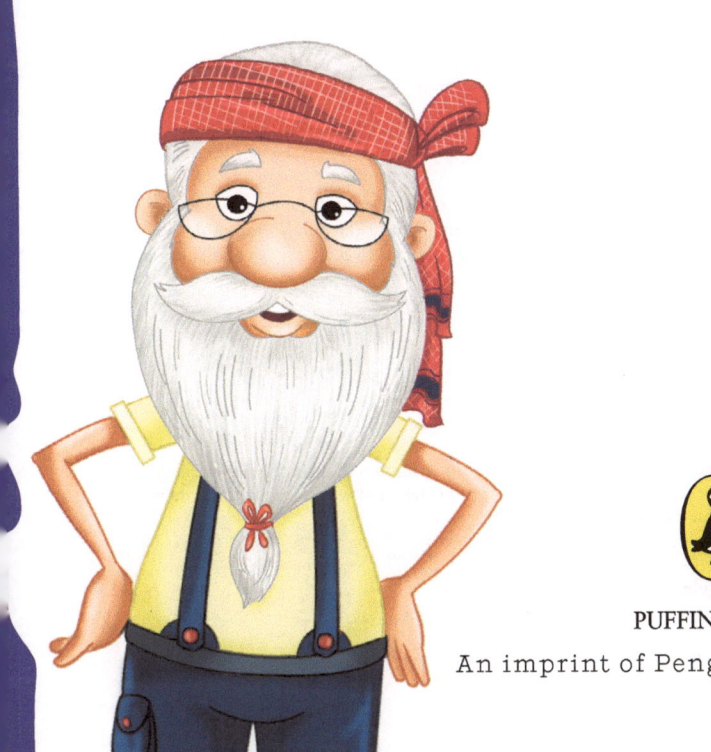

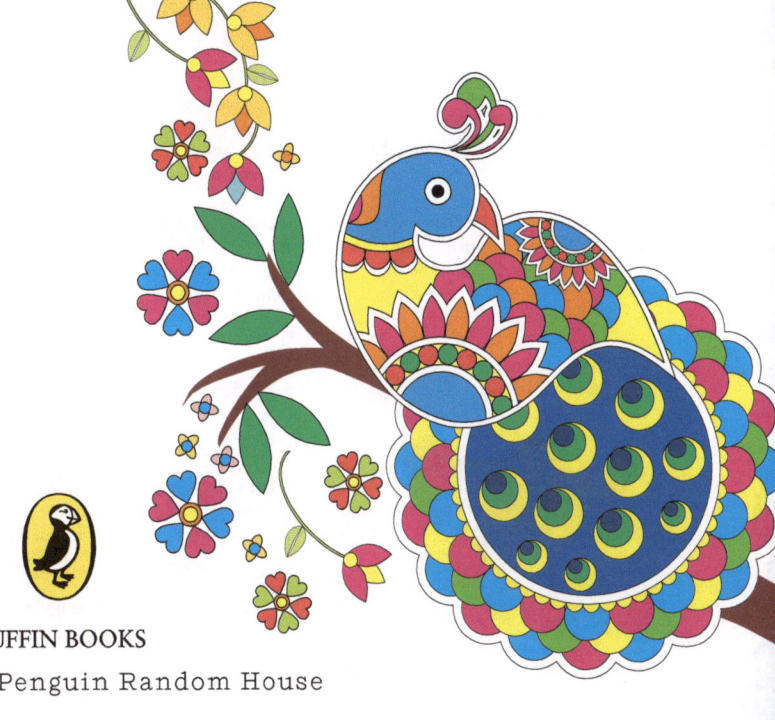

PUFFIN BOOKS

An imprint of Penguin Random House

PUFFIN BOOKS

USA | Canada | UK | Ireland | Australia | New Zealand | India | South Africa | China | Singapore

Puffin Books is part of the Penguin Random House group of companies whose addresses can be found at global.penguinrandomhouse.com

Published by Penguin Random House India Pvt. Ltd
4th Floor, Capital Tower 1, MG Road,
Gurugram 122 002, Haryana, India

First published in Puffin Books by Penguin Random House India 2018

Text, design and illustrations copyright © Quadrum Solutions Pvt. Ltd 2018
Series copyright © Penguin Random House India 2018

Picture Credits

P 7: Sena village, Bodh Gaya, Bihar (© Hideyuki KAMON (originally posted to Flickr as Mountain of Ashram) [CC BY-SA 2.0 (https://creativecommons.org/licenses/by-sa/2.0)], via Wikimedia Commons); P 8: A local house in Gaya, Bihar (Maythee Voran/Shutterstock.com); P 10: A Bihari farmer (Travel Stock/Shutterstock.com), A farm in Bihar (clicksabhi/Shutterstock.com); P 16: Coin from Samudragupta's rule (© I, PHGCOM [GFDL (http://www.gnu.org/copyleft/fdl.html), CC-BY-SA 3.0 (http://creativecommons.org/licenses/by-sa/3.0/) or CC BY-SA 2.5-2.0-1.0 (https://creativecommons.org/licenses/by-sa/2.5-2.0-1.0)], via Wikimedia Commons); P 20: People travelling in an auto rickshaw in Muzaffarpur, Bihar (clicksabhi/Shutterstock.com); P 28: A house in Bihar (© Vikram (Own work) [CC BY-SA 4.0 (https://creativecommons.org/licenses/by-sa/4.0)], via Wikimedia Commons); P 29: A decorated house in Raxaul, Bihar (Travel Stock/Shutterstock.com); P 34: Sher Shar Suri's Tomb (© Apleeo (Own work) [CC BY-SA 4.0 (https://creativecommons.org/licenses/by-sa/4.0)], via Wikimedia Commons); P 38: Both pictures of Son Bhandar (©Aryan paswan (Own work) [CC BY-SA 3.0 (https://creativecommons.org/licenses/by-sa/3.0)], via Wikimedia Commons); P 39: Samwasaran (© Jain cloud (Own work) [CC BY-SA 4.0 (https://creativecommons.org/licenses/by-sa/4.0)], via Wikimedia Commons), Pawapuri Temple (© Photo Dharma from Penang, Malaysia (003 Gateway to temple) [CC BY 2.0 (http://creativecommons.org/licenses/by/2.0)], via Wikimedia Commons); P 40: A farm in Bihar (clicksabhi/Shutterstock.com); P 48: Paag (turban) (© Mithilapride (Own work) [CC BY-SA 4.0 (https://creativecommons.org/licenses/by-sa/4.0)], via Wikimedia Commons)

All rights reserved

10 9 8 7 6 5 4 3 2

The views and opinions expressed in this book are the author's own and the facts are as reported by her, which have been verified to the extent possible, and the publishers are not in any way liable for the same.

The information in this book is based on research from bona fide sites and published books and is true to the best of the author's knowledge at the time of going to print. The author is not responsible for any further changes or developments occurring post the publication of this book. This series is not a comprehensive representation of the states of India but is intended to give children a flavour of the lifestyles and cultures of different states. All illustrations are artistic representations only.

ISBN 9780143440871

Design and layout by Quadrum Solutions Pvt. Ltd
Printed at Repro India Limited

This book is sold subject to the condition that it shall not, by way of trade or otherwise, be lent, resold, hired out, or otherwise circulated without the publisher's prior consent in any form of binding or cover other than that in which it is published and without a similar condition including this condition being imposed on the subsequent purchaser.

www.penguin.co.in

This is a legitimate digitally printed version of the book and therefore might not have certain extra finishing on the cover.

Hello Kids!

I'm so happy you are reading this book. India is an incredible country and there are lots of things about it that we never get to hear about.

I discovered India because my father was in the Indian army. He was posted to many places all over India—and we dutifully followed him. Can you imagine that by the time I was in the tenth standard, I had changed nine schools? Of course it was hard making new friends almost every year, but the good part was that I got to live in so many places. Right from Kerala, where I was born, to Kashmir, Jhansi, Shillong, Chandigarh, Goa . . . the list is long.

Every time I go to a new place, I feel amazed at how different each state is from the other—and yet, how similar. Did you know that we can see monuments from the Stone Age right here in India? Or that we have more than twenty official languages, and most Indians know three or four on an average? Or even that some of the world's most amazing scientific marvels were invented in India?

Oh, there are many, many, many fun and fantastic things about the states of India, which we simply must get to know.

So get your backpack ready, get set to meet some new friends and join me on a fun trip as we **DISCOVER INDIA, STATE BY STATE**.

I hope you enjoy reading this book as much as I have enjoyed writing it. I would love to hear from you. So do write to me at sonia.mehta@quadrumltd.com.

Lots of love,
Sonia Aunty

Mishki and Pushka have come to visit Earth from their home planet, Zoomba. They have never seen such an amazing place. Zoomba doesn't have trees and mountains and rivers like Earth does. But the people look exactly the same. When they come to Earth, they meet a sweet old man whom they call Daadu Dolma. Daadu Dolma shows them all the wonderful places in India and tells Mishki and Pushka all about them.

Mishki and Pushka can't believe what they see. They have seen a lot of Earth, but they have never, ever seen a place like India.

They are off to explore India state by state :)

Mishki

Mishki is a curious little girl. She is always asking loads of questions. On her home planet, she is always getting into trouble for poking her nose into things that are not her business.

Pushka

Pushka is Mishki's brother. He loves adventure. He is always ready to try a new challenge. Whether it's climbing a mountain, or diving into a cold, cold sea, he is up for it.

Daadu Dolma

Daadu Dolma is a wise old man who has lived on Earth longer than the mountains and seas. No one knows quite how old he is, but he certainly has been around. He knows everything about everything.

Mishki and Pushka have a lot of questions for Daadu Dolma.

'Where are we going now, Daadu? What kind of clothes should we carry?' Mishki asks.

'And what should we expect? Will we see wildlife? Should we carry our cameras?' adds Pushka.

'One at a time,' laughs Daadu. 'We are going to Bihar, a state that has an old, old history. So yes, carrying your cameras is a must. And yes, we will see some wildlife for sure. Are you ready to go?'

'Yes, yes, yes!' shout Mishki and Pushka. They love to travel and are super excited because they are

OFF TO BIHAR!!!

Land ahoy!

Yes, Pushka. Bihar is a landlocked state. This means that it has land on all sides. It shares one border with a foreign country. Come, let's explore Bihar.

Daadu, I can see land everywhere and no sea.

NEIGHBOURS APLENTY

Bihar has plenty of neighbours to keep it company. West Bengal, Uttar Pradesh and Jharkhand are its neighbours. Bihar shares its northern border with the country of Nepal. No time to feel lonely here!

ON THE MAP

To see exactly where **Bihar** is on the map of India, go to http://www.mapsofindia.com/maps/india/india-political-map.htm

FLAT AS FLAT CAN BE

Bihar is mostly made of flat plains. And what lovely plains! Most of Bihar is made up of the famous Indo-Gangetic plain. India's most famous river, the Ganga (also known as the Ganges), divides the state into two parts—the North Bihar Plains and the South Bihar Plains. It's only in the north that Bihar has a tiny bit of mountainous area, where it touches the foothills of the Himalayas. This is called the Terai region.

Did you know?

The south of Bihar includes a part of the Chota Nagpur Plateau. Most of this plateau is now in the state of Jharkhand.

RIVER RUSH

Apart from the magnificent Ganga, considered one of India's most holy rivers, there are many other rivers that generously water the plains. The Ghaghara, the Gandak, the Bagmati, the Kosi and the Mahananda are some rivers that rush down the Himalayas.

Some call the Kosi the 'Sorrow of Bihar' because it floods so often and causes a lot of destruction to crops and homes in the plains.

Sandy soil

Clay-like soil

MUDDY STUDY

Bihar has some colourful soil. Most of the north has sandy soil. The south is a little different. It has many small hills with dark, clay-like soil. Small rivers meander through this region, watering the land as they go. Not all the soil is fertile, but farmers still try to grow things, even in the most difficult parts.

SHAKY GROUND

Parts of Bihar are prone to earthquakes because they lie in what is called the Himalayan earthquake zone. There have been some earthquakes that have caused a lot of destruction to people's lives.

HOT, WET AND COOL

Bihar has three clear seasons. A hot, hot summer, when you feel like a baked potato; a rainy season that can leave you soaked in minutes; and a gentle winter, which is the best season of all.

People build homes with simple material so that they can be rebuilt easily.

A LITTLE BIT OF FOREST

Only a small part of Bihar has forests and this part is at the foothills of the Himalayas. There are some valuable trees, like the sal, banyan, bamboo, bodhi and palmyra trees.

Sal is the most commonly found tree.

WHAT'S ODD?

Pushka thinks that each row has a word that doesn't belong in it. Can you help him find them?

| CLAY | MUD | BRICK | GOLD | SOIL |

| SUMMER | WINTER | DESERT | AUTUMN | MONSOON |

| PEEPAL | BAMBOO | BANYAN | ROSE | PALMYRA |

Bihar has some breathtaking landscapes of dense forests.

WONDROUS WILDLIFE

The deeper forests in Bihar have some wonderful wildlife. You might see Bengal tigers, leopards, elephants and many types of deer too! Be careful while you walk along the Kosi though—a crocodile might just snap at you. There used to be a large population of a bird called the Adjutant stork, but now there are very few of them left.

CROP HOP

Nearly half of Bihar is covered in farmland. The changing weather patterns have demanded that farmers get creative, so there is a mix of dry and wet crops that are grown here. Rice is the largest crop, followed closely by wheat, corn and barley.

HEALTHY HO!

Bihar has plenty of healthy and yummy fruit and vegetable farms. Mangoes, lychees and bananas are the most grown fruits. One of India's best types of potato, called the seed potato, is grown here. These potatoes make the best chips ever!

Farmers here have three harvest seasons, when different crops are sown and reaped.

Entire families pitch in and help on farms.

FUN FACTS

State animal
Gaur

State tree
Peepal

State bird
Indian roller

State flower
Kachnar

Bihar celebrates Sparrow Day on 20 March every year because sparrows are dwindling in number.

MIXED-UP GRID

This word grid has five animals from Bihar and five things that grow in Bihar. Can you help find them?

Q	B	A	R	L	E	Y	E	S	A
L	E	O	P	A	R	D	G	F	C
W	E	R	T	Y	U	D	E	E	R
W	E	R	L	Y	C	H	E	E	O
E	L	E	P	H	A	N	T	O	C
A	M	A	N	G	O	Y	U	I	O
S	D	F	T	T	I	G	E	R	D
G	W	H	E	A	T	G	H	J	I
R	I	C	E	A	S	V	B	K	L
B	V	C	X	X	C	V	M	L	E

CITY CITY BANG BANG

Bihar has some of India's most historic cities—they're now very busy. Come, let's visit a few.

MUZAFFARPUR

Some people call this large city 'the lychee kingdom'— that's how famous its lychees are. It's a very large commercial centre and is known for its universities.

Digha–Sonpur Bridge, Patna

PATNA

This is Bihar's capital city. It was once called Pataliputra. There are many stories behind its name. One of them is that a king named Putraka built this city for his queen, whose name was Patali. When they had a son, he named the city Pataliputra (*putra* means 'son' in Sanskrit). Sitting on the banks of the Ganga, Patna is now one of India's most crowded cities.

Ruins of the Nalanda University near Bihar Sharif

BIHAR SHARIF

This city has an incredibly long history, over millions of years old. It has many Buddhist, Hindu, Jain and Islamic landmarks. Wow! That means there must have been important people from all these religions living here centuries ago.

GAYA

This is one of Bihar's most historic cities. According to Hindu mythology, Lord Ram and his wife, Sita, visited Gaya to perform the last rites of Ram's father, King Dasharatha. It is also an important Buddhist pilgrimage centre. It is one of Bihar's largest cities and a major tourist attraction.

DARBHANGA

This busy city is a major medical hub with lots of well-known hospitals. In the age of the Ramayana, it is said to have been the capital of Mithila, the kingdom Sita was from.

HAJIPUR

This is known to be one of Bihar's fastest developing cities. Apart from being a busy industrial centre, it's known for the bananas it produces. What a contrast!

RIGHT MATCH

Can you match the city with what it is known for?

Bihar Sharif	Ram and Sita visited this city
Hajipur	Bihar's capital
Gaya	Many religious landmarks
Patna	Known for bananas

Long, long ago

Daadu, it seems like the history of Bihar is really interesting. Do we need a time machine to go back and observe it?

Ha ha! A time machine would have been wonderful. But even without one, we can visit the past and learn all about Bihar's amazing history. Come along, let's get going.

LEGENDS AND MYTHOLOGY

Bihar's history is intertwined with India's mythology. Lord Ram's wife, Sita, they say, is a daughter of Bihar. Her father, Janak, had a kingdom called Mithila, which included many parts of Bihar. Even the author of the Ramayana, Sage Valmiki, is said to have lived in this region for a part of his life.

Indian mythology is full of amazing stories that grandparents pass on to their grandchildren.

SAME OR DIFFERENT?

Mishki wants to draw a portrait of Sage Valmiki, who wrote the Ramayana. So does Pushka! Can you help them find two identical drawings of Sage Valmiki?

A   B   C   D

BIRTHPLACE OF RELIGIONS

Gautam Buddha is believed to have achieved enlightenment in Bihar, in the city of Bodh Gaya. Bhagwan Mahavir, who founded Jainism, was also born in Bihar. And that's not all! Guru Gobind Singh, the tenth and last Sikh Guru, was born here and attained sainthood in this region.

Guru Gobind Singh

ANCIENT KINGDOMS

One of the earliest mentions of Bihar's history talks of several ancient kingdoms that happily coexisted on the vast plains of Bihar. Magadha, Anga and Licchavi were some. The rulers of these kingdoms were wise, and they built systems that were very advanced. It was in the Magadha Empire that Buddhism was born.

THE MAURYAN EMPIRE

Chandragupta Maurya, who was expanding his kingdom, ruled this region for many years. He had a wily minister, Chanakya (also known as Kautilya, the author of *Arthashastra*), who advised him on how to deal with Greek invaders. He not only managed to keep them at bay but also made sure that the Greeks coexisted peacefully with the Mauryan Empire for many years.

Alexander the Great led the Greeks on their expansion spree. One of his lieutenants, Megasthenes, lived in Pataliputra for many years. He wrote about how grand life was at the time.

ASHOKA THE GREAT

Yet another Mauryan king, Emperor Ashoka, changed the face of Bihar and the rest of India. A fierce warrior, Emperor Ashoka fought many battles to grow his kingdom. During one of them, he saw so much bloodshed that he was dismayed. He converted to Buddhism and began to spread Buddha's message of peace.

A coin from the Gupta period

Did you know? It was during the Gupta rule that the decimal system in mathematics was developed.

THE GUPTAS

The Gupta dynasty, led by King Chandragupta I and his son Samudragupta, ruled over Magadha after the Mauryans. During the Gupta rule, astronomy, science, mathematics and metallurgy advanced tremendously.

POWER TO WOMEN

Even in ancient times, the people of this region were very progressive and gave a lot of importance to women. It was here that Amrapali, a famous courtesan, wielded tremendous power. So much so that Gautam Buddha refused the invitations of several princes but made sure he met her.

EDUCATION FOCUS

The Guptas also established a university at Nalanda. It was one of the best universities of its time and imparted higher education.

HISTORY MYSTERY

Pushka has the names of these historical figures all jumbled up as usual. Can you help him unjumble them?

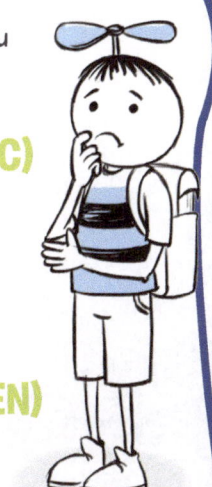

◆ A wily minister in Chandragupta Maurya's court _____ **(AYAHAKNC)**

◆ The sage who wrote the Ramayana _____ **(KIIMVLA)**

◆ The Greek conqueror _____ **(ADRELXAEN)**

◆ The foreigner who wrote about Pataliputra _____ **(SMEETHGASEN)**

◆ A famous courtesan _____ **(PRMAAALI)**

END OF AN ERA

The golden age of Bihar's history came to an end when invaders from the Middle East overcame the ruling kingdoms. These invaders were subsequently overthrown by the Mughals, who established themselves over much of India, including the region of Bihar.

A CHALLENGER OF THE MUGHALS

The Mughal Empire changed the very history of India.

There was only one man who successfully challenged the might of the Mughals. He was an Afghan ruler named Sher Shah Suri. He defeated the Mughal emperor Humayun and ruled this region for many years. He was a fierce warrior but also a good king.

THE BRITS ARRIVE

All this while, the British had been slowly and steadily taking over India. They had colonized the entire country. During this period, Bihar was a part of the region called Presidency of Bengal. Then, the British decided to merge it with Orissa (now called Odisha) and make it a separate province.

The British arrive in India

A FIERCE FIGHT FOR INDEPENDENCE

The Indians were not happy being under British rule. The British had enforced many rules and laws that were unfair to the Indians, so they began to fight for their independence. Many people from Bihar played a major role in the freedom struggle.

We demand independence!

A simple farmer called Raj Kumar Shukla met Gandhi, the leader of the Indian freedom struggle. Shukla told him about how farmers in Bihar were being mistreated by the British in a place called Champaran. Gandhi organized a massive revolt called the Champaran Satyagraha. It became the first of many important struggles that made the British eventually go away.

INDEPENDENCE AT LAST

Finally, in 1947, the British went away, giving India its independence. At that time, Bihar was not a separate state; it was a part of the Presidency of Bengal. It was only some years later, in 1956, that the government of India decided to reorganize the states based on language. That is when Bihar became a proper state.

Nothing like being free!

Talk time

The history of Bihar is very cool. Imagine, people were so clever in those days. I'd like to meet some people now. Can we, Daadu?

Yes, after you've learnt a little bit of the language.

HINDI WITH A TWIST

The official language of Bihar is Hindi, but there are many dialects. Some of these languages have evolved from old languages spoken thousands of years ago, like Maithili, Magadhi and Bhojpuri. Bhojpuri is perhaps the most popular, so let's learn some phrases in it.

- Welcome = Aain naa
- How are you? = Kaa haal ba?
- What's your name? = Tohar naav kaa ha?
- I don't know = Humke naikhe maaloom
- Do you speak Bhojpuri? = Tu bhojpuri bole la?
- Yes, a little = Haan, tani tani
- Sorry = Maaf karin
- Thank you! = Dhanvaad!
- I love you = Hum tohse pyaar kareni

WORD MATCH

Can you match the English words to their Bhojpuri translations?

Yes, a little | Sorry | Welcome | What's your name? | How are you?

Maaf karin | Kaa haal ba? | Tohar naav kaa ha? | Haan, tani tani | Aain naa

A peep into their life

Daadu, since it is said that so many religions were born here, are people very religious?

Some people are, Mishki, and they celebrate many festivals. Of course, they enjoy music and dance too. Come, let's explore Bihar's culture.

FESTIVE FERVOUR

Most of the festivals in Bihar revolve around nature. People worship the sun, the moon, trees, water and even many animals.

SAMA CHAKEVA

This festival is celebrated because of the story of a girl called Sama, whose father turned her into a bird in a fit of anger. Her brother, Chakeva, helped her become a human again through prayer and sacrifice. This festival celebrates the love between brothers and sisters. Young girls make idols of Sama and Chakeva and pray for their brothers' well-being.

IN WORSHIP OF THE SNAKE GODDESS 🌺

Bihula is a festival during which devotees worship the serpent goddess Manasa. Legend says that Manasa came to Earth to punish a man who did not believe in her. But, eventually, she ended up forgiving him. During this festival, people read out this story of Manasa. Bihula teaches people to be kind to snakes, even though they can be dangerous.

CELEBRATING THE RAIN

Madhushravani celebrates the rain. Devotees carry pots of water and empty them over the *Shiv lings* in Lord Shiva temples, thanking the lord for the rain that helps their crops and praying for a good monsoon the next year as well. Many other states celebrate this festival too!

A Shiv ling is a symbol of Lord Shiva.

WORSHIPPING THE SETTING SUN

Chhath Puja is one of Bihar's biggest festivals. All over the world, Bihari people get together to celebrate the setting sun. But here's a twist—the sun must be near water. So, during Chhath Puja, which happens twice a year, you'll see enormous crowds of people collecting near beaches and waterfronts to pray to the sun as it sets.

MUSIC FOR EVERY OCCASION

RELIGIOUS MUSIC

There are singers in this state called *bhajaniayas* and *kirtaniyas*, who sing devotional music. These singers are hugely popular, and whenever there is a religious event, people ask them to perform. Everyone joins in and they sing together.

Bihar has meaningful folk music. Here are some beautiful folk songs that people sing.

Sohar — Sung when a child is born

Sumangali — Sung at weddings

Ropni geet — Sung when paddy is sown

Katnee geet — Sung when paddy is cut

Beer kunwar — War songs

GOING CLASSICAL

Bihar isn't only about folk and religious music. Classical music has been an important part of this region for centuries. Ancient kings and emperors were great music lovers. They encouraged singers to perform in their courts. They even invited artists from other states. Because of this, some wonderful styles of classical music as well as singers and musicians have come from Bihar.

CRAFTY CREATIVITY

The people of Bihar seem to be really good with their hands too. They make amazing things with bamboo, brass and wood. A style of painting called Patna Kalam is very famous. They also create lovely lacquer bangles and stunning applique work.

This painting is in the Patna Kalam style.

How colourful are the Madhubani designs!

MADHUBANI PAINTINGS

This is one of Bihar's most famous art forms. Originally, village women used natural colours from vegetables to paint intricate patterns on the walls of their homes. This style of painting became so popular that now Madhubani paintings are done on paper and fabric too. They decorate the walls of homes around the world.

HIDDEN WORDS

Madhubani is such a big word! There are many small words hidden in it. How many can you find? Mishki has made one.

MADHUBANI

__BAN__ ____ ____ ____ ____

____ ____ ____

CHANCE TO DANCE

≥YAY≤ Now's your chance to dance! And there are some lovely dance forms to choose from. Come, let's decide which ones we want to do.

PAIKA

This is a sort of war dance in which dancers wield weapons and use them as props. Performers wear dhotis and colourful turbans. Holding wooden swords and shields, the dancers enact a mock fight in tune to the beat of an instrument called the *mandal*.

JHIJHIYA

It's time for this dance when there is no rain. Through the dance, people persuade Lord Indra, the god of rain, to shower their fields. This dance is performed mainly by women.

What a nice way to ask for help!

BIDESIA

This is like a dance drama, during which performers enact issues in their daily lives, like the conflicts between rich and poor people or women being left alone when their husbands go to work in big cities. In ancient times, women didn't perform this dance, so the men dressed up as women to play their parts too!

KAJARI

This is a monsoon dance. People perform this dance for an entire month, celebrating the rain. All the songs are in praise of Mother Earth for being so generous and giving them so much. It's a happy dance and makes you feel like joining in.

TWIN OFFERINGS

Mishki and Pushka are preparing their offering for Chhath Puja. Help them find the identical plates.

Bricks and stones

Ooh! Are we going to go into people's homes now? Daadu, I simply love to see how people live.

We will definitely see some homes, but we won't disturb the people who live there. We'll just understand what kind of houses are built in Bihar.

VILLAGE HOUSES

For centuries, Bihar has been a mainly agricultural state. Many of Bihar's people live in its thousands of villages. The villagers build their homes themselves using local materials, which, in Bihar, are mud, bamboo and clay. They also like to celebrate together. That is why village houses usually have large courtyards. Often, the houses collapse due to wind and rain, and they have to be rebuilt frequently.

BATTLING THE WEATHER

Since Bihar can get very hot in summer, houses are built to keep the insides cool. They are built on a raised platform with small windows; this keeps the heat out. In fact, in some houses, there are no windows at all and the only opening is the door.

HOUSE BEAUTIFUL

People also make their homes pretty by painting the walls. They paint lovely patterns in the Madhubani style of painting. How nice it looks!

PAINTING FUN

Look at this lovely flower Mishki has drawn in the Madhubani style. Can you draw one too?

Draw here

Standing strong

Daadu, I can see many Buddhist and Jain monuments here. Why is that?

Gautam Buddha started Buddhism right here in Bihar. Emperor Ashoka built many monuments to spread the message of Buddhism. Jainism was also born here, so there are many Jain monuments too.

STUPA OF SARIPUTRA

When archaeologists excavated the ruins of the ancient Nalanda University, they came across this remarkable stupa. Sariputra, after whom the stupa has been named, was one of the Buddha's favourite students. Like the Buddha, he too achieved enlightenment. The entire site of the stupa has pillars and smaller stupas with carvings depicting the Buddha's life.

VISHNUPAD TEMPLE

Buddhists believe that Gautam Buddha meditated at this temple before he went to Bodh Gaya, where he achieved enlightenment. This lovely temple was built in memory of the Buddha. It has statues, engravings and stupas that people come from far and wide to see.

A World Heritage Site is so precious that we must protect and preserve it at any cost.

MAHABODHI TEMPLE

Here's a place every devout Buddhist wants to visit at least once. Right in the heart of this temple stands the Bodhi tree, where the Buddha achieved enlightenment more than 2500 years ago. It is said that Emperor Ashoka built this magnificent temple nearly 250 years after the Buddha passed on. This temple is a UNESCO World Heritage Site.

NALANDA UNIVERSITY

This is one of the world's oldest universities and its ruins can still be seen at Nalanda. The kings of the Gupta and Pala dynasties sent their learned citizens to study here, hundreds of years ago. It must have been a beautiful and vast place, because it is said that the area that has been excavated is not even ten percent of the whole university.

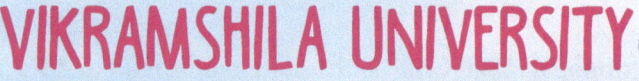

The ruins of Nalanda University, Bihar

VIKRAMSHILA UNIVERSITY

The ruins of another university, the Vikramshila University, tell us that people must have given a lot of importance to education. A king named Dharmapala from the Pala dynasty built this university that taught complex subjects, like philosophy, metaphysics, logic and theology. They say this university had more than a hundred teachers and a thousand students. Wow!

LION PILLAR

When Emperor Ashoka became a Buddhist, he erected many pillars across India that had a lion atop them. He also got sculptors to carve edicts of Buddhism on these pillars. It was so long ago that many of these have been destroyed. But about twenty still remain, and one of these ancient wonders is in Vaishali, Bihar.

An edict is an order or a commandment made by a person in authority, like a king or a president.

THE THAI MONASTERY IN GAYA

Buddhist monks built this monastery to meditate in. The monastery is built in a Thai architectural style and looks like a glowing gold and red gemstone. A spectacular idol of Gautam Buddha and many paintings and sculptures depicting his life make the monastery really beautiful.

JUMBLED WORDS

Pushka wants to remember all that he has learnt. But his words are mixed up. Can you help him unjumble them?

1. The monastery in _____ **YAAG** is beautiful.

2. A king from the _____ **ALAP** dynasty built the Vikramshila University.

3. Emperor Ashoka built many pillars across India with a _____ **IONL** atop them.

IBRAHIM BAYA MUKBARA

This is a tomb that is really worth seeing. It was built for a general called Ibrahim Malick, who was in the army of Mohammed bin Tughlaq (another warrior king who captured a large part of India at one time). Because it's built on a hill, the view from the top is lovely.

SHER SHAH SURI'S TOMB

This brave Afghani warrior ruled the region of Bihar for many years. People say he was a good king and a great builder as well. He built an entire city inside a magnificent fort. But one of his most amazing structures was his own tomb at a place called Sasaram. It has carved pillars and terraces that surround the actual tomb where Sher Shah is buried.

THE HEALING TOMB

The special thing about this tomb is that this is where one of India's first women Sufi saints is buried. (Sufism is a special kind of spiritual belief). Hazrat Bibi Kamal, it is said, had powers of healing. Even now, so many years later, people come to visit this tomb and believe that by praying here, their illnesses will be cured.

Looks peaceful!

CROSSWORD TIME

Pushka wants to see who finishes the crossword first. You can try too!

DOWN

1. A person who follows a special kind of spiritual belief.

3. The name of one of the world's first large centres of higher education.

4. A Buddhist structure in Bihar that is named after the Buddha's favourite student.

5. Where Sher Shah Suri and others like him are buried.

7. The place where a lovely Thai monastery is located.

ACROSS

2. A place of higher education.

6. This lion _____ has Emperor Ashoka's edicts on it.

8. His religion made Emperor Ashoka give up war.

9. Hazrat Bibi was a Sufi _____ .

TEMPLE BELLS

MUNDESHWARI DEVI TEMPLE

This ancient temple is dedicated to Lord Shiva and Goddess Shakti. People say that it is one of the oldest functional temples in the whole world. Thousands of devotees come to pray here.

> WOW! That makes it really old.

AJGAIBINATH

Here's a Shiva temple with a story. It is built near the Ganga. Legend goes that the Ganga was cursed by a sage called Jahnu. A king called Bhagirath prayed hard and released the Ganga from Jahnu's curse. A Shiva temple was built where the Ganga was released. Now, devotees throng here to pray and collect holy water from the Ganga.

UMGA TEMPLE

This is a temple built for an ancient goddess named Umga. It was built with local stone. It also has other idols, like statues of Ganesha and Shiva. You need to climb many steps up a hill to reach this temple.

SHADOW Bells

Mishki wants to ring all the bells in all the temples she has visited. Can you help her find the exact shadow of this bell?

A   B   C   D

PUNORADHAM IN SITAMARHI

The most famous thing about this temple is that this is where Sita (Lord Rama's wife) is said to have been born. Legend goes that King Janaka was once ploughing a field himself, to defy a famine his kingdom was facing. And there in the earth, he found a newborn baby—Sita. He brought her up as his own daughter. A temple was built in this spot.

IN THE FOOTSTEPS OF MAHAVIR

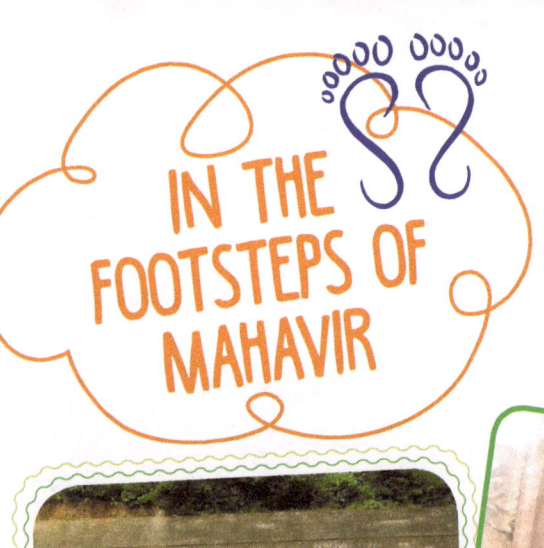

Lord Mahavir established Jainism in Bihar. Today, this religion is followed by millions of people across the world. Let's visit some places in Bihar that are important to Jains.

What detailed carvings!

This is the most typical pose that you will see Mahavir Bhagwan in.

SON BHANDAR

Son Bhandar means 'treasure of gold'. These are two rock-cut caves where the engravings of Jain saints (called Tirthankaras) are found. Legend goes that this was once the treasury of a king named Bimbisara and was filled with precious gold. This is what has given these caves its name. This must have been a wonderful place to meditate.

NATHNAGAR

This gorgeous temple is where people believe the twelfth Tirthankara, named Vasupujya, was born. It has a majestic dome and an ornate ceiling on which scenes from Mahavir's life are crafted out of shards of glass.

PAWAPURI TEMPLE

This is a really important place because this is where Jains believe that Tirthankara Mahavir attained nirvana. There is a beautiful white marble temple in the middle of a large lotus tank here. There is even a cremation ground, where people say Mahavir was cremated. Devotees collect soil from this ground and believe it is blessed soil.

SAMWASARAN

Some Jains believe that it was here that the last Tirthankara, Mahavir, gave his first and last sermon. There is a pristine white marble yard from where a flight of stairs take you to the shrine of this Jain saint.

Working hard

We've seen that in the past, the people of Bihar built many universities. But what do they do for a living now?

Oh, people do many things. They work on farms, in factories and in businesses. There are some traditional businesses too that people have been running for generations. Come, let's see what kind of work people do in Bihar.

FARMER, FARMER, WHAT DO YOU GROW?

As we saw, nearly half of Bihar's population is busy with farming activities. Apart from rice, wheat and pulses, people grow sugarcane and jute. Oh, and there are lychee farmers who grow this delicious fruit too!

LINKED TO FARMERS

Connected to agriculture, people work in sugar mills, silk-production factories and jute mills too. These businesses are linked to agriculture because they depend on what farmers produce.

FACTORY FACT

The government is trying to encourage people to set up more factories here so that more people will get employment. The main factories are of rubber, plastics, transport equipment, textile, chemicals, leather and dairy.

RHYME TIME

Pushka and Mishki are busy writing a poem about this state. But they want words that rhyme with 'Bihar'. Can you give them suggestions? They need at least seven.

BIHAR

_____   _____

_____   _____

_____   _____

_____

MOVIE TIME

Bhojpuri movies are very popular. In fact, there is a large film industry, where many people work as actors, directors, writers and so on.

Mishki, come! Let's enjoy a Bhojpuri movie.

Oh, I'd love to!

Yum yum yum

Oh, thank heavens! It's time to eat. Daadu, what's the food of Bihar like? Will I like it?

You like everything, Pushka.

Both of you are going to love the taste and variety of the food in Bihar. Some dishes are similar to the dishes in neighbouring states. Let's get to it; I can see that Pushka is starving.

FOOD HABITS

Bihari cuisine is intriguing. Though there are so many rivers, it's not known for its fish dishes. Instead, the best-known dishes in Bihar are vegetarian. There are loads of pickles. And many kinds of snacks and sweets too!

SATTU KA SHARBAT

People usually have this refreshing drink in summer. It's made of sattu, which is a kind of flour. Bet you never imagined a drink made of flour!

DAAL PITHA

You could call this Bihar's version of momos. This delicious dish is made of rice flour, stuffed with lentil paste, steamed and then eaten with pickle. It's a great breakfast dish, but you could eat it at any time.

KHAJURIA

Here's a divine snack. It's made with wheat flour and jaggery, then fried to crunchy perfection. Eat it any time hunger attacks because it is easy to cook and easier to eat. This dish is also called thekua and is served as prasad during Chhath Puja.

GHUGNI

This is a delightful main course that's made of soaked black chickpeas, cooked in a gravy. People eat it with puffed rice or parathas.

Looks delicious!

LITTI CHOKHA

This dish is similar to dal baati from Rajasthan. Litti is a baked wheat dumpling. It's filled with sattu (that's fried gram flour) and had with chokha—a heavenly mix of spicy vegetables. The dollop of ghee adds that extra something. It's delicious and very, very filling.

KHAJA

This is a speciality of a village called Silao, which has an ancient tradition of making khaja. Now everyone in Bihar loves it. It's a sweet dish made of flour, sugar and ghee. People make it in many different shapes, but the rectangular shape is the most popular.

A lot of street sellers fry mounds of khaja on roadsides. Looks lovely!

Yummmmmy! There's a rumble in my tummy!

BELGRAMI

Here's another mouthwatering sweet. It's made from cheese, sugar and ghee, and you simply cannot have just one!

PEDAKIYA

If you have a sweet tooth, Bihar's the place for you. Here's another sweet delicacy that the town of Chhapra is famous for. This dish is made of semolina and sugar. But here's the twist—it's wrapped in thin flour leaves and then deep fried.
Oh! Sounds sinfully lovely.

KHEER MAKHANA

No visit to Bihar is complete without this lovely pudding. It is made of makhanas (lotus seeds), milk and sugar. It's the best way to finish off a satisfying meal.

TILKUT

Gaya is where this crisp sweet is believed to have originated. It's made of sesame seeds and sugar. Other states like Maharashtra also have something similar but with different names. Either way, this crunchy sweet tastes yummy!

BALUSHAHI

A lot of states take credit for this amazing dessert. But the people of Bihar believe it was first created in the town of Bhagalpur in this state. It's basically a fried flour dumpling that is soaked in sugar syrup. It's shaped like a doughnut. People across India adore this. You will too!

The balushahi from different states taste different too!

CRACK THE FOOD CODE

Pushka and Mishki want to send a secret message to Daadu. Can you crack the code?

| 1 = W | 2 = L | 3 = D | 4 = E | 5 = V | 6 = O | 7 = T | 8 = F | 9 = H | 0 = R |

1 4   2 6 5 4   7 9 4

___ ___   ___ ___ ___ ___   ___ ___ ___

8 6 6 3   9 4 0 4

___ ___ ___ ___   ___ ___ ___ ___

What to wear?

Daadu, do the people today dress very differently from ancient times?

Oh yes! People now dress for convenience. In ancient times, clothes were more elaborate. Come, let's see some styles.

Paag

DIFFERENT STYLES

Bihar has a wonderful mix of people from many different religions. This is why people have variations in their clothes.

HOW THE MEN DRESS

Men in Bihar traditionally wear a dhoti and kurta. Muslim men prefer lungis. Both dhotis and lungis are long pieces of cloth, just draped differently. In some parts of Bihar, men wear a turban called a *paag*. It's an important part of their clothing because it indicates stature.

ALL DRESSED UP

For weddings and festivals, men and women here love to dress up. Men like to wear a type of coat called a sherwani. They even have special jewellery. Cool!

DELIGHTFUL DRAPES

Many women wear saris that they drape elegantly around themselves. Bihar is famous for handwoven textiles. *Tussar* is a type of silk that is popular. When women are all dressed up, they wear tussar silk saris.

Chandrahar

Young girls here dress like other girls all over the world. They wear jeans, T-shirts or salwaar kameezes. But during festivals, they love wearing traditional clothing.

Sikri

A tussar silk sari

JEWELLERY JOY

Oh, the women here love their jewellery. Some of their accessories have lovely names, like *chandrahar*, *tilri*, *panchlari*, *satlari* and *sikri*.

Autograph, please?

With so many religions being born here, Bihar must have some really great people, Daadu.

Yes, that's for sure. But these people are not only from religious fields. There are artists, musicians and sportspeople too. Let's meet some of these famous people.

ARYABHATTA

He was an ancient astronomer and scientist, who developed many theories that we follow even today. It is believed that he was the first to come up with the concept of zero and place values. He was such a genius that it is said he wrote his first work, called *Aryabhatiya*, when he was just twenty-three years old.

India's first satellite, Aryabhatta, was named after this genius mathematician.

CHANAKYA

He was a minister in the court of Chandragupta Maurya. Some historians believe that it was his thinking and strategy that helped the Mauryan kingdom reach such heights. He was a clever and learned man, who even wrote a book on economic policy—*Arthashastra*. He was also known by some as Kautilya.

VIDYAPATI

He was a great poet from Mithila, who wrote long and elaborate poetry about Lord Krishna and Radha. Many of these poems are still much loved and recited.

DR RAJENDRA PRASAD

He was a freedom fighter and went on to become India's first president.

JAYAPRAKASH NARAYAN

He was an important political leader whose thinking inspired many. People called him Loknayak (hero of the people). He played an important part in India's freedom struggle.

BISMILLAH KHAN

He was an amazing *shehnai* player, whose ancestors were musicians in the royal courts of Bihar. He made the shehnai popular. It is now associated with wedding music.

GANGA DEVI

She was believed to be a pioneer of the Madhubani style of painting. She was a folk painter but brought a contemporary touch to this classical style of painting.

RAMDHARI SINGH DINKAR

This amazing poet was called Rashtra Kavi (national poet). He was also a great humanist—his ideas benefitted humanity.

RAVI KISHAN

He's a Bhojpuri film star, and the people of Bihar are quite crazy about him! He's acted in many Bhojpuri films and some Hindi films too.

SUBODH GUPTA

He is a modern painter, sculptor and photographer whose works are now famous across India and the world.

WHO'S NOT IN PLACE?

Pushka is very impressed with these famous people. He wants to decide what he should be when he grows up. But he is confused about all the different professions there are. Can you help him find which job is odd in each row?

| ACTOR | DIRECTOR | SCULPTOR | PRODUCER |

| CRICKETER | FOOTBALLER | SWIMMER | POET |

| POET | AUTHOR | PAINTER | SONGWRITER |

Once upon a time . . .

Thank you, Daadu. That was a wonderful experience. Do we have time for a story from Bihar? Or do we have to leave?

THE STORY OF FAITH AND WILL

We always have time for a story, Pushka. Especially from Bihar because there are some lovely folk tales and mythological tales as well. Come, I will tell you a folk tale from Bihar.

There once lived a poor man named Kalia in the village of Rajgir. He had a daughter called Kamala. Kamala was not just pretty but also very clever. One day, Kamala was walking home from the woods, when she saw a young man rush past her.

'Where are you off to in such a hurry?' she asked him.

'I must reach the Ganga for a holy dip before the sun sets,' the young man replied.

'Well, the Ganga is still a mile away and the sun is about to set. Can you see that muddy pond there? Have faith that it is the Ganga and take a dip in it,' Kamala suggested.

The youth was puzzled, but he did as she said. He plunged into the muddy pool with full faith. When he emerged, his hands were full of jewels.

'See,' Kamala said with a smile, 'faith can make anything possible.'

The young man fell in love with Kamala. His name was Govind. He wanted to marry Kamala and asked her father for permission to do so. Here too Kamala had a suggestion.

'Ask my father for a cow, a dog and a parrot that he owns. I do not want anything else,' she whispered to him. Govind did as he was told. He didn't know that all these creatures had special powers.

Kamala and Govind were married and happily lived together in Rajgir. One day, the parrot came squawking and sat on Kamala's shoulder. It whispered something in her ear. The parrot had special powers that let it spy on Lord Indra's court. Lord Indra was the god of thunder and storms, and also the god that ruled all other gods. People said he had a short temper, and everyone was afraid of him.

'Lord Indra is going to send rain only to plots of land that are barren, where crops cannot grow,' it said. 'All our plots are barren. This is an opportunity for us to grow crops on the barren land.'

Kamala got thinking. She asked the dog to dig up all the barren land. Then, she asked the cow to fill the earth with manure. And finally, she told Govind to sow grains in the field. She told all the other people who had barren land to do the same.

Soon, it began to rain. It rained only on the barren plots of land. To Lord Indra's surprise, all those plots grew fine, lush crops. Govind and Kamala became rich. And so did the villagers of Rajgir.

Lord Indra was puzzled when he saw this. He had wanted to play a trick on these people, but how had they caught on? He had no idea about the parrot. He decided to send rats to these plots to eat up the crops.

Once again, the clever parrot rushed to Kamala and whispered Lord Indra's plan in her ear.

Kamala got to work at once. She told Govind to organize an army of cats to drive away the rats. Lord Indra was annoyed. He decided to send a storm to spoil the grain. But once again, Kamala was prepared.

She told Govind and the villagers to dig a deep moat. Then, she told them to place all the harvested grain deep inside the moat and cover it all with heavy stones through which water could not pass.

Once again, Lord Indra's plan was foiled. When the storm arrived, the grains stayed safe. But this time, instead of being annoyed, Lord Indra was impressed. He blessed Kamala and the entire village, and from that day on, the village never wanted for anything. All the villagers became prosperous thanks to Kamala's will and faith.

People say that the moat still exists in Rajgir, reminding everyone who sees it that if they have faith and will, they can overcome anything!

TRAVEL DIARY

Have you enjoyed this trip to Bihar with your friends Mishki and Pushka—and, of course, with Daadu Dolma?

Now you can make your own Bihar diary. And if you ever visit Bihar, make sure you take pictures and put them in the photo box.

The first place I would visit in Bihar:

_____

If I were a farmer, I would grow:

_____

The one dish I am definitely going to eat:

_____

The monument I think is the most interesting:

_____

The one famous person from Bihar I would love to meet:

_____

I think the most interesting historical figure from Bihar is:

_____

The festival from Bihar that I think is the most fun:

_____

The five words that I think describe Bihar the best are:

_____

_____

_____

_____

_____

My Bihar memories:

ANSWERS

page 9 WHAT'S ODD
GOLD, DESERT, ROSE

page 11 MIXED-UP GRID

Q	B	A	R	L	E	Y	E	S	A
L	E	O	P	A	R	D	G	F	C
W	E	R	T	Y	U	D	E	E	R
W	E	R	L	Y	C	H	E	E	O
E	L	E	P	H	A	N	T	O	C
A	M	A	N	G	O	Y	U	I	O
S	D	F	T	I	G	E	R	D	D
G	W	H	E	A	T	G	H	J	I
R	I	C	E	A	S	V	B	K	L
B	V	C	X	X	C	V	M	L	E

page 13 RIGHT MATCH
Bihar Sharif—Many religious landmarks;
Hajipur—Known for bananas;
Gaya—Ram and Sita visited this city;
Patna—Bihar's capital

page 15 SAME OR DIFFERENT?
A and C are identical.

page 17 HISTORY MYSTERY
Chanakya, Valmiki, Alexander, Megasthenes, Amrapali

page 21 WORD MATCH
Yes, a little—Haan, tani tani; Sorry—Maaf karin;
Welcome—Aain naa; What's your name?—Tohar naav kaa
ha?; How are you?—Kaa haal ba?

page 25 HIDDEN WORDS
Here are some of the words you can form: and, bad, bid,
bud, dam, dim, din, dub, had, ham, hid, him, hum, mad,
man, mid, mud, nib, band, damn, dumb, lamb, maid, main,
mind, numb

page 27 TWIN OFFERINGS

page 33 JUMBLED WORDS
GAYA, PALA, LION

page 35 CROSSWORD TIME
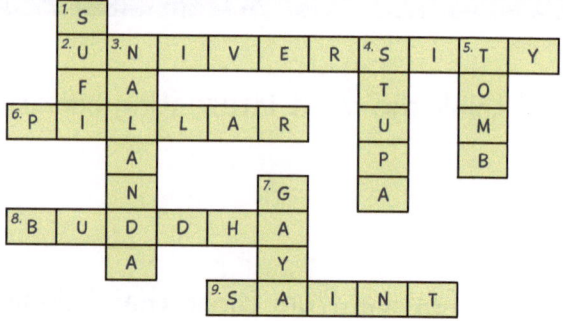

page 37 SHADOW BELLS
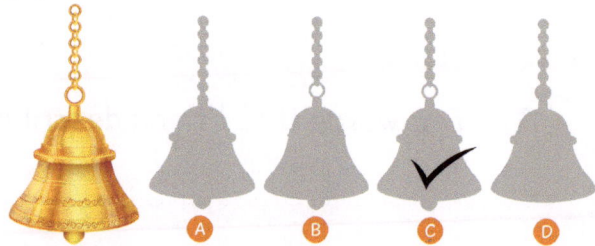

page 41 RHYME TIME
CAR, FAR, STAR, JAR, BAR, PAR, MAR, AJAR,
TAR, SPAR

page 47 CRACH THE FOOD CODE
WE LOVE THE FOOD HERE

page 53 WHO'S NOT IN PLACE?
SCULPTOR, POET, PAINTER